DEAR COLORING ENTHUSIAST,

WELCOME TO A WORLD OF CHRISTMAS ORNAMENTS!

LET YOUR CREATIVITY SHINE AS YOU BRING THESE FESTIVE DESIGNS TO LIFE WITH YOUR COLORS.

HAPPY COLORING!

WE HOPE YOU'VE ENJOYED THIS ENCHANTING JOURNEY THROUGH THE WORLD OF CHRISTMAS ORNAMENTS.

YOUR CHOICE TO COLOR WITH US MEANS A LOT. MAY THE MAGIC OF THESE ORNAMENTS FOREVER INSPIRE YOUR HOLIDAY SPIRIT.

UNTIL NEXT TIME, MAY YOUR DAYS BE FILLED WITH WARMTH AND VIBRANT COLORS.

If you enjoyed this book, check out more of our products on the Kiddo Notes author's page on Amazon.

Made in United States
Troutdale, OR
11/25/2024

25262063R00058